Also by Carol Ann Duffy in Picador

The World's Wife

Feminine Gospels

Rapture

New Selected Poems

Mrs Scrooge

Love Poems

The Other Country

Another Night Before Christmas

The Bees

The Christmas Truce

Wenceslas

Mean Time

AS EDITOR

Hand in Hand

Answering Back

To the Moon

Bethlehem

A Christmas Poem

Carol Ann Duffy

Illustrated by Alice Stevenson

PICADOR

With thanks to Nia Dryhurst

First published 2013 by Picador
an imprint of Pan Macmillan, a division of Macmillan Publishers Limited
Pan Macmillan, 20 New Wharf Road, London N1 9RR
Basingstoke and Oxford
Associated companies throughout the world
www.panmacmillan.com

ISBN 978-1-4472-2612-3

1 3 5 7 9 8 6 4 2

A CIP catalogue record for this book is available from the British Library.

Manufactured in Belgium by Proost

Visit *www.picador.com* to read more about all our books
and to buy them. You will also find features, author interviews and
news of any author events, and you can sign up for e-newsletters
so that you're always first to hear about our new releases.

For Camilla Elworthy

BETHLEHEM

A mild dusk; the little town
                        snaked
on the edge between desert and farmland;

camel prints in the sand
            like broken hearts;
the call and response of sheep
            among dry shrub.

To the West,
                    the whispering prayer of olive groves;
incense of rosemary, cedar, pine, votive
on purpling air.

Everyone there who had to be there.

The lamps lit; all Bethlehem
full;
every cave stabled with beasts, jostling for hay
in the fusty gloom;

every room
peopled and packed from rafter to floor;
barley bread in the ovens rising . . .

8

and a girl's hands
                              at an open door,
her blade halving a pomegranate,
its blood on her pale palms . . .

a voice from an alleyway chanting a psalm.

The moon rose; the shepherds sprawled,
shawled,
a rough ring on sparse grass, passing
a leather flask.

From the town,
a swelling human sound; cooking smells braiding the hour
as lambs and fishes spat in the fires.

A hundred suppers –

                        honey, fig, olive, grape,
set before stone-cutter, potter, tent-maker, maid,
nurse, farmer, child.

Young wine in the old jars, yellow and cold.

The Inn bulged; travellers boozed,
                              bawled,
bragged, swapping their caravan tales; money-lenders
biting their gold coins;

        painted women
dancing on tables; mules brayed
outside in the stable;
a youth in the courtyard strummed on a harp.

The sweating Innkeeper shouted and served;
his wife counting the heads,
then making up beds on the flat roof,
in the vine-covered yard.

Above, bright news in the sky, arrived, a star.

The small hours; all living souls
                              slept
or half-slept; the night fires smouldering low
out in the scrub;
the olive oil cooling in clay lamps;
a goatherd snored in the straw
                              between two goats.

Silent night;
a soft breeze from the desert
laying a dusting of sand on the dark road,
blessing the homes.

A donkey's slow, deliberate hooves on the stones.

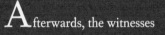

Afterwards, the witnesses
                              spoke
of a singing boy, an angel,
walking the fields in the hour before dawn,
winged in his own light;

of how the shepherds fled from the sight,
lambs in their arms.

And some swore, on their lives,
on their children's lives,
that they saw an olive tree

                                    turning to pure gold . . .

that the moon stooped low to gape at the world.

What's certain – the time and place:

                              heard,

three crows from the cockerel;

                         seen,

the stable behind the Inn;

present,
animals, goatherd, shepherds, Innkeeper, wife . . .
then the small, raw cry of a new life.

And one wept at a miracle; another
was hoping it might be so;
                              others ran,
daft, shouting, to boast in the waking streets.